5.50

Ben Nicholson : the Meaning of his Art

Ben Nicholson

the meaning of his art

J. P. Hodin   1957

ALEC TIRANTI   LONDON

Contents

Made and printed in the United Kingdom

Acknowledgments

The illustrations contained in this volume, with two or three exceptions, have not previously been published. Thanks and appreciation are due to all those whose works are here reproduced, to the artist himself for selecting the picture material, and to Mr. E. C. Gregory for permission to use the source material listed in the two volumes published on the artist by Lund Humphries.

Ben Nicholson : the meaning of his Art

To find the true relationship of sensations is to unveil the similarity of these sensations in the realm of the senses, with a definite primary notion of pure harmony which rests deep in the soul of man ; is to recognize it and bring it to light.

Johann Kepler, *Harmonices Mundi.* 1619.[1]

The culture of the industrial age, contemporary culture, in which life and thought have been reshaped and defined by modern science and technology, is only in an early stage of crystallization. It is an age of basic changes—this, our Aquarian age, the age of the common man—revolutionised in all its aspects : religious, philosophical, social, aesthetic. Its future is uncertain and as yet an idea, a concept rather than a reality. This concept, this idea, however, is the fruit of the creative genius of modern man who with his background of traditional values established in the Greco-Christian era, is unceasingly active in conceiving notions and formulations of new values ; values which are becoming the world-view and the style of modern man. Man has taken up new positions even in his relationship to the universe. For the moment, it is the uncertainty of

1

finding a way to translate those venerable age-old traditional values into the universal image of a unified mankind whose life is dominated by science, rather than the certainty of the new as a whole which dominates the spiritual scene of our day. Only a very few people are able to make a clear cut, a definite decision towards the new. Clarity of ideas, a pioneer spirit endowed with a sense of courage and adventure, a certain quality of temperament—for seen in historical perspective the concepts of a truly modern man are different from those of any European man hitherto—and a firm spiritual conviction which can be called religious without being dogmatic and churchbound, are necessary preconditions for such a direction towards a new world-view and a new style.

As an artist, Ben Nicholson was privileged to take this decisive step very early in his career. It happened at a time when new stylistic formal concepts and elements were still in an early stage of development, awaiting the creative spirit to be cast into shape and to be organised into a meaningful unity. We recognise in Ben Nicholson's work a contribution towards that serene harmony and beauty which is a symbol and an expression of a new humanism, a new spiritual order. It is classic in its vision for it has striven for and achieved the balance of the opposing forces of life ; it is mature because it has been victorious over the disturbing and disturbed state of mind of present-day man—a state of mind whose uncertainties are caused both by its dissociation from the primary forces of creation and by its willingness to

2

accept a modern way of life. This uncertainty, this dissociation makes for anxiety. ' Fear and Trembling ' are the key-note of modern man's disharmony with himself and the Universe. It seems a paradox that the world of modern scientific man should be shaken by his inability to come to terms with the eternally unchangeable and with the time-bound new, the logical outcome of evolution and our fate. Here then, before our eyes opens up this Nothingness, this Chaos which has replaced the old canons, paralysing the mind and undermining reverence for life, soiling the miracle of creation with its Nihilism and reducing mankind to a rationalistic antheap governed by the machine and by a narrow-minded materialism.

But man cannot live for long in dread and chaos ; and although it may as a pastime be attractive to the intellectuals, the romantics and the decadents, truly creative man, obeying an unwritten moral and aesthetic code, will make every effort to lighten darkness, to cure decay, to form order out of chaos. This always was and will remain the calling of the truly great and responsible. A modern artist, such as Ben Nicholson, will conceive his work in this positive spirit and offer to his own time a vision of primary significance. What did the critics and the traditionalists want to achieve when defining his artistic integrity by way of futile puritanistic formulae ? The act of creation and its myth has been repeated in a twofold way in Nicholson's work. First, in its elemental significance. ' In the beginning God created the Heavens and the Earth. And the Earth was *without form* and void ; and darkness was upon the face of the deep.'[2] Here for the first time man has conceived creation out of Nothingness. In all the myths prior to it, there is always something out of which the world has been created.[3] The Babylonian myth of creation, for instance, relates how in the beginning the mighty God Marduk fought and killed the great dragon Tiamat, an embodiment of the primeval watery chaos, and how after his victory he created the present heaven and earth by splitting the huge carcass of the monster into halves, setting one of them up to form the sky, while apparently using the other half to fashion the earth.[4] The notion of Nothingness out of which something is created is of essential interest for our time. Only Jewish and Greek imagery was of importance in the formation of our traditional concepts. According to Hesiod ' first verily existed Chaos.'[5] Ovid tells us that ' before there was any earth or sea, before the canopy of heaven stretched overhead, Nature presented the same aspect the world over, that to which man has given the name of Chaos. This was a *shapeless* unco-ordinated mass, nothing but a weight of lifeless matter, whose ill-assorted elements were indiscriminately heaped together in one place.'[6]

Creation is the primary act which ends chaos and brings forth life and order. Artistic creation is a phenomenon of elemental creation in that it creates a human analogy. And therein it is both less and more than elemental creation. More because it continues elemental creation, for everything is perpetually in change and the human impulse is needed not only to witness but to

4

fulfill the primary act for every generation. Our generation has suffered under the onslaught of its own creativeness in the field of science and technology. By the dissolution of its old established standards it has returned to the notion of Nothingness and with it to the feeling of dread, i.e., to spiritual chaos which is an image of primary chaos. ' Dread reveals Nothingness.' And : ' Nothing is that which makes the revelation of what–is as such possible for our human existence.' So says Heidegger. ' Nothing not merely provides the conceptual opposite of what–is but is also an original part of essence.'[7] Dissociated man has lost his central point. Dissociated modern man, who has forsaken and negated God, tries to find his central point not in God but in the direction towards God. His creative energy is engendered by the faith that it might once more bring about the unity of man and creation, the fulfillment of his spiritual task without which he cannot live. He thinks and shapes in the light of creation which is in itself the annihilation of chaos, of Nothingness, of dread. For this reason he proceeds from the fundamental to counter chaos with the primary experience of truth. For this reason also the squares and circles in the middle phase of Ben Nicholson's work must be looked upon as the elements of a new order.

Can squares and circles express the unfathomable quality of existence ? Yes, in a certain sense they can, as we shall see. Can they replace the infinite shapes of life, the ciphers of Being ? No, and they are not intended to do so. The critic who experiences in these ' geometric ' forms bloodless cerebral constructions presented as the only subject-matter of art is mistaken. On the other hand : these forms are not so meaningless nor their function so simple. The true subject-matter of such compositions in Ben Nicholson's work is order and harmony, is cosmos. Before we enter this point, however, let us investigate more closely why such forms appear in the art of our time and what constitutes the thought process which has brought them about. There is no doubt that scientific thought and method have a powerful influence on the rationalisation of modern art.[8] This is so not only in the sense that they invade its realm, which indeed they do in many respects, but also in that the artist realises that there are and always have been present in art as they are present in philosophy and in life itself, many agents which escape intellectualisation. Let us reverse the problem by saying that apart from the intuitive and ineffable quality each work of art also contains the ingredients of creative criticism which is an intellectual factor. We speak of the influence of scientific thought and method in its proper sense only when, as in our modern art and in the art of the Renaissance, the laws of composition and representation are dominated by a scientific thought process, such as Renaissance perspective and anatomy (observation). The triangular composition in the plane is a dominant feature of the High Renaissance, as are also other more complicated constructions. The lines of perspective into the depth amount to triangles, the base of which is the lower edge of the picture and its apex the one or two vanishing points. Triangles and circles are, however, well hidden behind the arrangements of the subject-matter proper. They are the scaffolding of the Renaissance picture. As in modern times, there were minor artists also in the Renaissance on whose minds the rational problem exercised a stronger influence than their talent could apply. Ben Nicholson is an artist whose art is not dominated by the rational application of a geometric principle only. It is with its help that he expresses a credo for modernity. He is too sensitive an artist to be ruled by narrow rational programmes ; his whole personality is involved in an unceasing process of creation. That is also why the first geometric figures, strictly speaking, appear only in his later work (about 1937), while his paintings show a pre-occupation with squares and circles as early as 1923–24, in his painted reliefs in 1933. This must have a meaning.

Mondrian, to whose style Nicholson's geometric compositions and reliefs have a great affinity, restricted himself, in his mature work, to a few elements : the straight line and the right angle ; in shapes to the rectangle and the square, in colour to the primary hues red, blue and yellow. Behind this seemingly ascetic scheme there was a religious fervour, a burning faith in modern man's own culture. They speak to us from his own life as an artist and from his writings. The elements were few but they were pure. They were elements of an aesthetic law and order, of a revolutionary modern architecture which was expressive of present-day civilisation. They also voiced the essence of Mondrian's philosophy which was the philosophy of liberation from all that was particular and the verification of all that has become universal. 'All are running counter to the culture of the past, the culture of the particular form, and all are living already within the culture of the new era, the culture of the pure relationships.[9]

It is, above all, through architecture that the spirit of the time manifests itself aesthetically in any civilisation. It was thus in the Gothic period, in the Renaissance and in the Baroque. It is so also in modern times. Until a new architecture has taken shape which is congruent to its own time, to its spirit, its materials, its working processes, we cannot speak of a new culture having been established. The principle of geometry in modern architecture goes back as far as to the late eighteenth century. (Ledoux and Boullée.) The basic forms of geometry were proclaimed the basic forms of architecture.[10] This must be considered an outcome of the philosophy of the Encyclopaedists who intellectually prepared the French revolution and the era of reason.

Quite logically, therefore, we find that the de Stijl movement in Holland (founded in 1917) accepted two elements as the fundamental basis of its work, whether in painting, architecture or sculpture, furniture or typography : in form, the rectangle ; in colour, the primary hue. The circle or semi-circle was included in the work of the *Bauhaus* and of the early Le Corbusier (Savoy House, Passy-sur-Seine, 1929–30) ; combined forms appeared later.[11]

8

In the stylistic decadence and academic sterility of the nineteenth century, geometry had to render the first service of a new orientation. Historically seen, it has always fulfilled such a function.[12] It is here that lies the importance for our time of Cézanne's famous sentence : ' You must see in nature the cylinder, the sphere, the cone.'[13] What it meant was the re-orientation toward form and the constructive idea establishing it.

The great and decisive event in the history of the modern movement was Cubism, not Fauvism. Cubism constitutes the dividing line up to which each new direction in art was preparation only—the pre-Cubist phase—the post-Cubist phase being the new synthesis, the new style. Since the Quattro- and Cinquecento, the fifteenth- and sixteenth-century Renaissance, no attempt had ever been made in European art to replace its particular concept of picture-making, i.e., the Renaissance laws of composition and construction. Now the time was ripe again and it is the merit of Picasso (and Braque) to have dared to enter this adventure in which at last new means of rendering space and representing objects were sought. In the process, which can be understood as a parallel to the deductive thought process in science, Cubism has confronted modern man with an art as new as modern science and philosophy are new. The feeling of liberation and of a novel beginning was tremendous. The freedom of the modern artist to express his experiences independently of any canonised formula, led to art forms which, generally called abstract and non-figurative, non-objective or pure plastic, are, in

9

fact, ideational art forms as opposed to representational ones. Picasso himself has pushed his adventure as far as abstraction, and this already in 1910 (Nude, Cadaqués). Without him the whole further development in art is unthinkable. In connecting the Cézannesque notion of geometrising with a thrust into the primitive experience of art, a wholeness of concept was reached which could counter that of the Renaissance. All pre-Renaissance art movements, especially the primitive ones in Europe and elsewhere, provided the new soil of tradition for the modern style. Ben Nicholson, who belongs to the second generation of the post-Cubist period,[14] is nearer to Braque's lyricism, especially in his still-lifes, than to Picasso ; and if we add Mondrian, Ozenfant's and Le Corbusier's Purism, we have accounted for the ancestors of Ben Nicholson's geometric oeuvre. As in the art of Picasso, there is also in Ben Nicholson's art a trend towards the primitive. It seems that only when both are fused will they satisfy the modern artist's urge for new roots. Ben Nicholson's primitivism or naivism is related to that of Christopher Wood and the Cornish fisherman Alfred Wallis and finds its most eloquent application in the rendering of landscapes (mainly Cornish, also Cumbrian, Yorkshire, Provençal, Tuscan). A new element, not evident in Cornwall, enters particularly into the landscape drawings from Italy : the grandeur of architecture with its powerful conception of volume, its refinement of detail, and its wealth of decoration.

Why did Ben Nicholson choose the square (the rectangle and the related L-shape) combined with the circle as elements of his paintings and reliefs in that middle period between 1934–45 which we call the *Euclidian, Architectonic and Platonic* phase ? And do the square and the circle perhaps signify in themselves something which goes beyond geometry ? From a geometric point of view and according to Euclid's Elements, the circumference of a circle is a plane curve such that all points in it have the same distance from a fixed point in the plane, its centre. A rectangle is contained by the two sides which contain one of its right angles.[15] As we have already mentioned, Ben Nicholson did not start with strictly geometric forms. But when we read in Klee's *Pedagogical Sketchbook* that the mobility agent of a line is a point (in fact, the lead point) shifting its position forward ; or when we study Kandinsky's *Punkt und Linie zur Fläche* (Point and Line to Plane)[16] we realise that theoretically they started with Euclid (the path of a moving point is a line, the path of a moving line is, in general, a surface, the path of a moving surface is, in general, a solid. Euclid). Ben Nicholson, one generation later, did not need to go back to Euclid. He accepted the geometric form established already by Picasso, Mondrian, van Doesburg, Malevich and others, as a basic form of modern art and architecture, expressive of a modern ordering spirit and primary for a contemporary creativity. When the empirical rules of Egyptian geometry which arose from the need of surveying the lands inundated by the Nile floods

11

(geo—earth, metron—a measure) were developed by the Ionic School, they passed in their new shape (sixth century B.C.) into the care of the Pythagoreans. From this time, geometry exercised a powerful influence on Greek thought. Pythagoras sought the key to the universe in arithmetic and geometry, and the Platonists, later on, by accepting in part the Pythagorean cosmology, made the study of geometry preliminary to that of philosophy. It is in the relationship between the geometric shapes in the framework of a picture surface, in the sensibility of the artist in arranging them and in applying colours, that the limitless possibilities of a cosmos governed by harmony to modern man were revealed.

Geometry has its primary source in the observation of nature itself. Sun and moon are circles and so their tracks appear. The pupil of the human eye is a circle, and a stone falling into water causes it to ripple in concentric circles. The cell of the honeycomb or minerals are polygonic ; the sea horizon is a straight line, and so is the flight of the wild geese. Primary experiences dwell in the human psyche as archetypal images (C. G. Jung). The eye itself has an ordering and creative faculty ; and according to *Gestaltpsychology* which has analysed this faculty, a small child will render a perceptual feature in the simplest possible way as long as it is not yet differentiated. And the circle is the simplest possible shape available in the pictorial medium.[17] While the Freudian analyst will emphasise the primary significance for the child's imagination of the mother's round breast, the Gestaltpsychologist will speak of the lever construction of the human body which favours curved motion and therefore the priority of the circular shape visually. Both are right in their own field of research. For the age of the Ionian philosophers, the sphere was the most accomplished mathematical body. That is also why they conceived the world as a sphere, for it was their conviction that it represented a cosmos, that is to say, a comprehensively built, ordered and harmonious world. The Pythagorean harmony was in a wider sense conceived as ' the state of a whole whose parts are related to one another in a proper ratio corresponding to a given norm.[18] To Kepler the circle was still the primary image of transcendental harmony.[19] When analysing the architecture of the primitives, v. Sydow established as its two main forms the hemospheric room in the form of the so-called beehive-hut—the floor of which is a circle—and the quadrangular structure ; and when speaking of the initial stages of the art of drawing of primitive peoples, he describes them as purely abstract plane figurations. There are, firstly the geometric round forms: circle, spiral ; and secondly the angular forms : rectangle, irregular angular forms and simple lines. Numerically, the round forms are in the majority.[20] To the medieval alchemist, the antique geometric problem of the Sophists of squaring the circle acquired a new significance. The squaring of the circle became a symbol of the ' opus alchymicum ' wherein the initial chaotic unity was dissolved into its four elements, fire, air, water and earth, and then again combined into a higher unity.

13

This higher unity was represented by a circle, the four elements by a square.[21] The Tibetan Mandala (Buddhist), which contains in the upper part of its rectangle the transfigured tranquility of the perfected ones and in the lower part the demonic motion of savage gods, shows in its centre a sharply delineated circle representing an intrinsic order.[22] To Jung, the alchemist's transmutation of base metals into gold signifies ' the transformation of the personality through the merging and the binding together of noble and base elements, the conscious and the unconscious ' ; and in a similar vein the Mandala is to him a symbol expressing the integration of the personality and the emergence of the self. The Mandala is, in fact, a design found in the art of virtually all peoples. It is based on a perfectly balanced square or circle in which the mid-point is given particularly great importance.[23] The Renaissance rediscovered the famous Vitruvian figure in which man's shape is conceived as a harmony measured by a circle and a square. Square and circle were the pure elements of Roman architecture,[24] and from their basic geometry quality alone we can grasp how differently from Gothic architecture it was conceived. One of the great themes of disputation at the Congress of Master Masons, held in Milan in 1386, was that ' Utrum ecclesia ipsa . . . debeat ascendere ad quadratum an ad triangulam '—whether the church should be built according to the law of the quadrangle or to that of the triangle.[25]

By using the square and the circle in a structural manner (it is a conceptual and formal, not a symbolic,

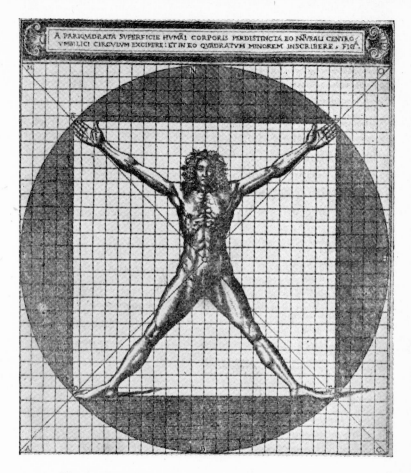

Vitruvian figure, from Cesariano's edition of Vitruvius, Como 1521

fact), Ben Nicholson gave expression not only to a primary human urge but his art thereby acquired the quality which in philosophy is generally attributed to the notion of the Platonic idea. Ideas were for Plato the incorporeal being defined through concepts. This was the first time that the principle of an immaterial reality had been stated in philosophy. The same relationship of similarity existing between the higher world of ideas and the lower world of appearances, between Being and Becoming, also exists between primary images and the forms shaped after their model. In a narrower sense and applying his theory of ideas to aesthetics, Plato spoke of a beauty which arouses pleasures in man that are relative neither to the satisfaction of a need nor to want nor to a mixture of both. They are produced by the enjoyment of the forms of plane and solid geometry. They give particular pleasure, unlike other pleasures, because they are not only relatively beautiful, like other things, but eternally and absolutely beautiful.[26] This Pythagorean element in Platonic philosophy exemplifies both idealogically and historically, as developed in this essay, the use of geometric forms in Ben Nicholson's art. And as in Plato's concept, the ideas, in addition to their interpretive value with regard to what is, serve as a standard of what ought to be, i.e., the ideas are transformed into ideals, so in the work of Ben Nicholson. The English artist confronts his own apocalyptic time not only with the idea but with the ideal of a new beauty, a new order, a new harmony. For this purpose he does not need a great deal of paraphernalia. A few geometric shapes, a few forms abstracted from everyday life, such as a jug, a goblet, a bowl, are sufficient. It is the spirit that purifies even the simplest, the commonest object. If this cannot be acknowledged as a moral power in a time which holds a record in dragging man down into cheap mass-produced shabbiness, if this cannot be considered the blossom of a religious conviction which approaches life with reverence, it speaks ill for the standard of present-day norms.

The still-life on a table is a theme which runs like a red thread through the entire work of Ben Nicholson. As in his white flat reliefs, Ben Nicholson found even here a personal form. Holding the balance between the Cubist and the Purist still-life, his serene and refined interplay of linear, plane and colour elements is quite original. As in the thirties the Cubist still-life was transformed into a completely flat pattern—the objects were then replaced by figurative playing cards—so in the forties the use of abstracted still-life motifs, inset like emblems into the background of landscapes, seemed to illustrate a dialectic process in which idea and reality, the ideal and the real, were confronted in their immutable interrelation. About 1945, a higher integration of the linear element takes place. The line begins to sing. More than the colour, more than the plane, it plays the role of the unifying, the spiritual element. A sublime harmony develops beyond the visible, forcing all the elements into a higher order. They now appear as though lit up by an inner immaterial light which feeds on the nostalgia for a human existence, brought into accord with that eternal will in which the beautiful, the meaningful and the good are one.

It was Pythagoras to whom has been ascribed that poetic notion of the harmony of the spheres which corresponds to the innate drive for harmony in the human soul. In its subtle integration of elements, Ben Nicholson's art borders on music, that noblest and purest of all arts, and canons have been detected in his work which coincide with those of the classical fugue-composition.[27] Work has also been in progress which shows how the classical laws of the Golden Section and of Vitruvius' and of Plato's concept of Dynamic Symmetry[28] are congruent with Ben Nicholson's way of composition, and how in his development the play of lines increasingly resembles those delicate figurations of higher geometry which express functions and relationships of the most complicated nature. Therefore, when we call this second and crowning phase in his development the *Pythagorean, Infinitesimal and Polyphonic* phase, we do no more than express in similes that unfolding of his classical style which is an analogy to the evolution of the Corinthian from the Ionic and the Doric order in Greek culture. England, and with it the whole present Euro-American culture, possess in Ben Nicholson the only classic artist whose work might be a forecast of future developments and a compass to harmony for the disturbed and distorted vision of to-day.

1937 (*painting*) private collection London (courtesy B.B.C.)

Literary Notes

1. Linz, 1619. Quoted from Johann Kepler. *Die Zusammenklänge der Welten.* Edited by Otto J. Bryk. Eugen Diederichs, Jena 1918.

2. Genesis, I, 1.

3. G. Scholem. *Schöpfung aus dem Nichts und Selbstverschränkung Gottes.* Eranos Jahrbuch, XXV, 1957.

4. James George Frazer. *The Golden Bough, A Study in Magic and Religion.* Part III ; The Dying God. Other creation myths see : Lewis Spence. *An Introduction to Mythology.* George G. Harrap, London 1921.

5. Hesiod. *Theogony,* 116. In : *The Poems and Fragments.* Done into English prose with Introduction and Appendices by A. W. Mair. Clarendon Press, Oxford 1908.

6. *The Metamorphoses of Ovid.* A New Translation by Mary M. Junes. The Penguin Classics, London 1955.

7. Martin Heidegger. *Was ist Metaphysik?* (1929). Vittorio Klostermann, Frankfurt a.M. 5th edition, 1949. English translation in: Martin Heidegger. *Existence and Being.* Vision Press, London, 1949.

On basis of Heidegger, J. P. Sartre reasons in a similar way . See : *L'être et le néant.* Essai d'ontologie phénoménologique, NRF, Librairie

Gallimard, Paris 1943. Chapter 1. L'Origine de la Negation. See also
Karl Jaspers. *Philosophie.* Springer Verlag, Berlin-Göttingen-
Heidelberg, 1932. Section : Sein und Nichts.

8. J. P. Hodin. *Art and Modern Science.* In : RIVISTA DI ESTETICA.
Istituto di Estetica dell' Universitá di Torino. Vol. I, No. 3.
September-December 1956. See also : Max Schoen. *The Intellectual
Temper in Contemporary Art.* THE JOURNAL OF AESTHETICS AND ART
CRITICISM, Vol. XV, No. 2, Cleveland, December 1956.

9. Piet Mondrian. *Art and Life,* 1931. In : H. L. C. Jaffé : *de Stijl,*
1917–1931. *The Dutch Contribution to Modern Art.* Alec Tiranti,
London 1956. See also : Michel Seuphor. *Piet Mondrian. Sa Vie,
Son Oeuvre.* Flammarion, Paris 1956.

10. The French architect du Fourny proclaimed in 1793 : ' L'architecture doit se régéner par la géométrie.' Analagously le Corbusier :
' Le reveil brutal en nous, parceque foudroyant des joies intenses de
la géometrie. . . .' In freedom man tends to pure geometry. Quoted
from : Hans Sedlmayr. *Verlust der Mitte.* Die Bildende Kunst des
19. und 20. Jahrhunderts als Symptom und Symbol der Zeit. Otto
Müller Verlag, Salzburg, 3rd edition 1948.

11. Alfred H. Barr, jr., *Cubism and Abstract Art.* The Museum of
Modern Art, New York 1936.
See also : H. L. C. Jaffé, op. cit. ; *Bauhaus* 1919–1928. Edited by
Herbert Bayer, Walter Gropius, Ilse Gropius, Charles T. Branford,
Boston 1952. And : Bruno Zevi. *Towards an Organic Architecture.*
Faber & Faber, London 1950.

12. See : Else Christie Kielland. *Geometry in Egyptian Art.* Alec
Tiranti, London 1951.
Rudolf Wittkower. *Architectural Principles in the Age of Humanism.*
Alec Tiranti, London 1952.
George Lesser. *Gothic Cathedrals and Sacred Geometry.* Alec Tiranti,
London 1957.

Leone Battista Alberti. *Ten Books on Architecture.* English translation by James Leoni. Edited by Joseph Rykwert. Alec Tiranti, London 1955.

13. John Rewald. *The Ordeal of Paul Cézanne.* Phoenix House London 1950.

14. The first generation of Kandinsky, Robert Delaunay, Sonia Delaunay, Jean Arp and Sophie Taeuber-Arp, Piet Mondrian, Van Doesburg, Malevich, Tatlin, a.o. is dealt with in Michel Seuphor's *L'Art Abstrait. Ses Origines, Ses Premiers Maîtres;* Maeght, Paris 1950. See also : Alfred H. Barr, jr., op. cit.
The first, second and third generations (including Tachism and Action Painting) are dealt with in Marcel Brion's *Art Abstrait*, Editions Albin Michel, Paris, 1956.
See also : Andrew Carnduff Ritchie. *Abstract Painting and Sculpture in America.* The Museum of Modern Art, New York, 1951, and : *The New Decade. 22 European Painters and Sculptors.* Edited by Andrew Carnduff Ritchie. The Museum of Modern Art, New York 1955.
On abstract theories, see : Frances Bradshaw Blanshard. *Retreat from Likeness in the Theory of Painting.* Columbia University Press, New York, 1945. And : Léon Degand. *Langage et Signification de la Peinture.* En Figuration et en Abstraction. Editions de l'Architecture d'Aujourdhui, Paris 1956. Also : Charles Biederman. *Art as the Evolution of Visual Knowledge.* Red Wing, Minnesota 1948.

15. See *Geometry* in THE ENCYCLOPAEDIA BRITANNICA. Vol. XI, 11th edition, London and New York 1910–11.

16. Paul Klee. *Pedagogical Sketchbook.* Faber & Faber Ltd., London [1952] (*Pädagogisches Skizzenbuch*, 1925, the 2nd of the 14 Bauhaus Books). Wassily Kandinsky. *Punkt und Linie zu Flache.* Albert Langen, Munich 1926.

17. Rudolf Arnheim. *Art and Visual Perception. A Psychology of the Creative Eye.* Faber & Faber, London 1956.

18. Heinrich Gomperz. *Die Lebensauffassung der Griechischen Philosophen und das Ideal der inneren Freiheit.* Eugen Diederichs, Jena 1904. Chapter : Vorsokratiker.

19. Johann Kepler, op. cit.

20. Eckart v. Sydow. *Primitive Kunst und Psychoanalyse.* Imago Bücher, X. Internationaler Psychoanalytischer Verlag, Leipzig-Wien-Zürich 1927.

21. C. G. Jung. *Psychologie und Alchemie.* Rascher Verlag, Zürich 1944.

22. Heinrich Zimmer. *Kunstform und Yoga im Indischen Kulturbild.* Frankfurter Verlagsanstalt, Berlin 1926.

23. C. G. Jung. *Die Beziehung zwischen dem Ich und dem Unbewussten.* Rascher Verlag, Zürich 1933.
And : Ira Progoff. *Jung's Psychology and its Social Meaning.* Routledge & Kegan Paul, London 1953.

24. See the paragraph on the Roman Ruins of Bath in the essay on Ben Nicholson in : J. P. Hodin. *The Dilemma of Being Modern. Essays on Art and Literature,* Routledge & Kegan Paul, London 1956.

25. Hans Karlinger. *Zahl und Mass. Zehn Aufsätze vom Ausdruck und Inhalt der gotischen Welt.* Gallus Verlag, Vienna 1944.

26. Plato. *Philebus,* 51. In : Dialogues. Translated by Benjamin Jowett. Clarendon Press, Oxford 1892.

27. See the paragraph on the Fugue in the essay on Ben Nicholson. In : J. P. Hodin. *The Dilemma of Being Modern,* op. cit.

28. Plato. *Theaetetus.* In : Dialogues, op. cit.
See also : E. Zederbauer. *Die Harmonie im Weltall, in der Natur und Kunst.* Orion Verlag, Vienna and Leipzig 1917. And : Matila Ghyka. *Geometrical Composition and Design.* Alec Tiranti, London 1956.

Biographical Notes

1. Ben Nicholson is the central figure of an artist's dynasty. Born on 10th April, 1894, at Durham, Bucks., he is the eldest son of the painter Sir William Nicholson and his wife, Mabel Pryde, herself a painter, and sister of the painter James Pryde.

Ben Nicholson was married to the painter Winifred Nicholson whose grandfather, the Earl of Carlisle, was a painter. Of the three children from this first marriage, Jake and Kate are painters. Of the three children from his second marriage, to Barbara Hepworth, Simon shows talent as a sculptor-painter and Sarah as a flautist.

2. In 1911 Ben Nicholson attended for one term the Slade School of Art in London. He spent the years between 1914–17 in London and North Wales, between 1932–39 in London and in 1940 he moved to Cornwall where he has since lived in Carbis Bay and St. Ives. His presence there contributed to the formation of a distinct art movement.

3. The pioneer character of his work in the modern English movement is well established. During 1925–36 he was a member of the ' 7 and 5 ' Group. In 1933 he joined ' Unit One ' and ' Abstraction-Création ' in Paris (until 1935). In 1937 he was co-editor with the architect J. L. Martin and the Russian constructivist Naum Gabo of CIRCLE,

23

International Survey of Constructive Art, in London. Personal contact with Mondrian and Hélion in Paris (1933) and with Gabo in London and Cornwall from 1936–45.

4. He has travelled much. We find him in Tours in 1911–12, in Milan in 1912–13, in Madeira in 1913–14 and in 1917–18 in Pasadena, California. From 1920–31 he lived partly in Castagnola, Switzerland, and partly in Cumberland and London. From 1950 onwards he has travelled often in Italy. In 1957 he visited the United States.

5. Ben Nicholson's first one-man show took place in 1922 at the Adelphi Gallery in London. In 1930 a one-man show took place at the Lefèvre Gallery where he exhibited subsequently in 1933, 1937, 1939, 1945, 1947, 1948, 1950, 1952 and 1954. Since 1954 he has exhibited regularly at the Gimpel Fils Gallery in London and since 1949 at the Durlacher Gallery in New York. In 1951 a one-man show was held at the Phillips Memorial Gallery in Washington, and in 1956 at the Galerie de France in Paris.

In 1934 his work was shown for the first time at the Venice Biennale; in 1935 in Brussels and in the same year in the ' These, Antithese, Synthese ' exhibition at the Kunstmuseum in Lucerne. In 1936 his work was represented in Amsterdam and in the ' Cubism and Abstract Art ' exhibition at the Museum of Modern Art in New York. In 1937 followed an exhibition in Philadelphia and in 1939 works of his were shown in the British section of the International Exhibition in New York, which later moved to San Francisco, Ottowa, Toronto, Montreal, Boston and Chicago.

In 1949 Ben Nicholson was invited to exhibit his work at the Salon des Réalités Nouvelles in Paris.

His first retrospective exhibition was organised by Philip Hendy in 1944 in Leeds City Art Gallery, Temple Newsam. The second retrospective exhibition was held in 1952–53 at the Detroit Institute of Art and the Walker Art Centre, Minneapolis. The third in the British Pavilion at the XXVIIth Venice Biennale (1954) from whence it moved to the Stedelijk Museum in Amsterdam, the

Musée Nationale d'Art Moderne in Paris, the Palais des Beaux-Arts in Brussels, the Kunsthalle in Zürich and the Tate Gallery in London. From 1935 onwards, Ben Nicholson has taken part in all important manifestations of non-figurative art in foreign countries. From 1954 the name of Ben Nicholson was finally established abroad as one of the leading artists of our time.

6. In 1952 he received the 1st prize for painting at the 39th International Exhibition at the Carnegie Institute in Pittsburgh. Two years later followed the Belgian Critic's Prize for the best exhibition in Brussels in 1954 (at the Galerie Apollo) and the Ulissi Acquisition Prize at the Venice Biennale of the same year. In 1955 came the ' Governor of Tokyo ' award at the 3rd International held in Japan and in 1956 the Grand Prix Award at the 4th International held at Lugano in Switzerland. The crowning honour received up to date is the 1st Guggenheim International Award won in a world-wide competition in 1956 and presented to the artist by the President of the United States. In 1957 he was awarded the International Prize for painting at the São Paulo Biennial.

7. In 1949 Ben Nicholson was commissioned to decorate two concave panels for the steamship *Rangitane* of the New Zealand Shipping Company, in 1951 to paint a mural for the Festival of Britain, and in 1952 to execute a wall painting for the Time-Life Building in London.

8. His works are included in the following *public collections :* Aberdeen Corporation Art Gallery ; Arts Council of Great Britain ; Birmingham City Museum and Art Gallery; City Art Gallery, Bristol ; British Council ; Glasgow Art Gallery and Museum ; Leeds City Art Gallery ; Manchester City Art Gallery ; Whiteworth Art Gallery, Manchester ; Laing Art Gallery, Newcastle-upon-Tyne ; Swindon Art Gallery ; Tate Gallery ; Ann Arbor, University of Michigan ; Albright Art Gallery, Buffalo, N.Y. ; Carnegie Institute, Pittsburgh ; Chicago Institute of Art ; Detroit Institute of Arts ; Grand Rapids Art Gallery, Michigan ; Walker Art Center, Minneapolis ; Guggenheim

Museum, New York ; Museum of Modern Art, New York ; Smith College Museum, Northampton, Mass. ; Philadelphia Museum ; San Francisco Art Museum ; Munson Williams Proctor Institute, Utica, N.Y. ; Phillips Memorial Gallery, Washington, D.C. ; National Gallery of Canada, Ottowa ; Toronto Art Gallery ; National Gallery of Victoria, Melbourne ; National Gallery of New South Wales, Sydney ; Musée des Beaux-Arts, Antwerp ; Palais des Beaux-Arts, Brussels ; Ohara Museum, Kurashiki, Japan ; Museu de Arte Moderna, Rio de Janeiro ; Galleria Internazionale d'Arte Moderna, Venice.

Selected Bibliography

WRITINGS BY BEN NICHOLSON

Ben Nicholson is not fond of theories and programmes.   He has
written only sporadically and reluctantly.
Aim of the Modern Artist. In : THE STUDIO, London, December 1932.
Statement in : *Unit One.* Cassell, London 1934.
Quotations. In : CIRCLE, Faber & Faber, London 1937.
Notes on Abstract Art.   In : HORIZON, London, October 1941 ;
    reprinted in *Art of This Century.* New York 1942, and in *Ben
    Nicholson. Paintings, Reliefs and Drawings.* Lund Humphries,
    London 1948.
Further Notes on Abstract Art. June 1948, in the same volume.
Defending Modern Artists. DAILY MAIL, London, 7th August 1951 ;
    reprinted in P.S.3, Penwith Society, St. Ives, Summer 1952.
Notes. Catalogue of Exhibition, Tate Gallery, London, June 1955.

WRITINGS ON BEN NICHOLSON

Books
Alfred H. Barr, jr.   Ben Nicholson. pp. 200–201. In : *Cubism and
    Abstract Art.* The Museum of Modern Art, New York 1936.

Herbert Read. Ben Nicholson. pp. 79–87. In : *A Coat of Many Colours. Occasional Essays.* George Routledge & Sons, London 1945.

John Summerson. *Ben Nicholson.* THE PENGUIN MODERN PAINTERS. Penguin Books, London 1948.

Herbert Read. Introduction to Volume I. *Ben Nicholson, Paintings, Relief and Drawings.* Lund Humphries, London 1948.

Herbert Read. *Contemporary British Art.* pp. 31 – 32, 44, 48. Penguin Books, London 1951.

Herbert Read. Ben Nicholson. pp. 216–225. In : *The Philosophy of Modern Art. Collected Essays.* Faber & Faber, London 1952.

Herbert Read. Introduction to Volume II. *Ben Nicholson, Work since* 1947. Lund Humphries, London 1956.

James Thrall Soby. Ben Nicholson. pp. 130–133. In : *Contemporary Painters.* The Museum of Modern Art, New York 1949.

Andrew Carnduff Ritchie. *Sculpture of the Twentieth Century.* pp. 29, 155, 230, 336. The Museum of Modern Art, New York 1952.

Will Grohmann. *Zwischen den beiden Kriegen.* p. 222. Vol. III. Kunst und Architektur. Suhrkamp Verlag, Munich 1953.

Werner Haftmann. Ben Nicholson. pp. 455 and 517 in Vol. I, and p. 503 in Vol. II. Of : *Malerei im 20. Jahrhundert.* Prestel Verlag, Munich Vol. I, 1954 ; Vol. II, 1955.

Frank McEwen. Ben Nicholson. p. 209. In : *Dictionnaire de la Peinture Moderne.* Fernand Hazan, Paris 1954.

Patrick Heron. Ben Nicholson. pp. 185–191. In : *The Changing Forms of Art.* Routledge & Kegan Paul, London 1955.

Hans Vollmer. *Allgemeines Lexikon der Bildenden Künstler des XX. Jahrhunderts.* E. A. Seemann Verlag, Leipzig 1956. Vol. 3, pp. 476–477.

J. P. Hodin. Ben Nicholson, The Pythagorean. pp. 106–119. In : *The Dilemma of Being Modern.* Routledge & Kegan Paul London, 1956.

John Rothenstein. Ben Nicholson. In : *Modern English Painters. Lewis to Moore.* pp. 260–282. Eyre & Spottiswoode, London 1956.

Paul F. Damaz. *Art in European Architecture.* pp. 86–147. Reinhold, New York 1956.

Bernard S. Myers (ed.). *Encyclopedia of Painting.* p. 362. Hutchinson & Co. London 1956.

Andrew C. Ritchie. *Masters of British Painting* 1800–1950. pp. 118–125. Museum of Modern Art. New York 1956.

Marcel Brion. *Art Abstrait.* pp. 280–286. Albin Michel. Paris 1956.

Michel Seuphor. *Dictionnaire de l'Art Abstrait.* Fernand Hazan, Paris 1957.

Articles and Catalogue Prefaces

Paul Nash. *A Painter and a Sculptor,* WEEK-END REVIEW. p. 613. 19th November 1932.

Adrian Stokes. *Ben Nicholson's Painting,* THE SPECTATOR. p. 517. 17th October 1933.

Geoffrey Grigson. *Henry Moore and Ben Nicholson,* THE BOOKMAN. p. 106. November 1933.

Jan Tschichold. *On Ben Nicholson's Reliefs,* AXIS. pp. 16–18, No. 2, 1935.

John Summerson. *Abstract Artists,* THE LISTENER. pp. 574–575, March 16th 1939.

J. L. Martin. *Architecture and the Painter, with special reference to the work of Ben Nicholson,* FOCUS, pp. 60–67, No. 3, 1939.

E. H. Ramsden. *Ben Nicholson, Constructivist,* THE STUDIO. pp. 179–181. December 1945.

Humphrey Slater. *A Note on the Importance of Ben Nicholson,* POLEMIC, pp. 49–51, No. 2, 1946.

Charles Etienne. *Peinture et Culture Anglaise.* Catalogue of Exhibition ' Jeune Peinture en Grande-Bretagne,' Galerie René Drouin, Paris 1948.

J. P. Hodin. *Ben Nicholson,* THE CORNISH REVIEW. pp. 83–88. Autumn 1949.

Eduardo Westerdahl. *Ben Nicholson y su arte,* INSULA. Madrid, 15th May 1950.

Patrick Heron. *Ben Nicholson,* THE NEW STATESMAN. p. 584. 17th May 1952.

The First (Second and Third) International Art Exhibition, Japan. The Mainichi Newspapers, Tokyo, 1952 (1953, 1955).

Frank McEwen. *Nouvelle Ecole Anglaise*, LE SOLEIL NOIRE. p. 160. Nos. 3 and 4, Paris 1953.

David Lewis. *Development of the Relief: Ben Nicholson and Pasmore*, ARCHITECTURAL DESIGN, pp. 48–49, No. 2, London, February 1954.

Eric Newton. *Ben Nicholson*, BRITAIN TODAY. p. 28. June 1954.

Herbert Read. Foreword to catalogue of exhibition in British Pavilion, XXVIII Biennale. Venice 1954.

Herta Wescher. *Ben Nicholson; Musée d'Art Moderne*, CIMAISE, No. 5. Paris 1955.

David Baxandall. *Peinture et Sculpture*, LES FORCES VIVES ANGLAISES. pp. 34–36. Paris, January-February 1955.

J. P. Hodin. *Ben Nicholson, peintre de l'equilibre et de l'harmonie*, LES BEAUX ARTS. pp. 1–3. Brussels, 4th March 1955.

Michel Seuphor. *Fernand Léger and Ben Nicholson*, ART-DIGEST. New York, 1st April 1955.

David Lewis. *Ben Nicholson*, ARTE VISIVE. pp. 5–7. No. 2. Rome 1955.

Gillo Dorfles. *L'Ultimo Ben Nicholson*, DOMUS. Milan 1956.

J. P. Hodin. *Ben Nicholson*, DIE KUNST. pp. 249–252. Munich, April 1955.

Léon Degand. *Ben Nicholson*, AUJOURD'HUI. p. 15, No. 7. Paris, March 1956.

R. V. Gindertael. *Ben Nicholson*, LES BEAUX-ARTS. Brussels, 20th April 1956.

Ben Nicholson—Profile. THE OBSERVER. London, 21st April 1957.

J. P. Hodin. Ben Nicholson Lauréat du Prix International Guggenheim. PRISME DES ARTS. pp. 10–12. No. 12. Paris 1957.

Printed by Portland Press Ltd., London. W.1.

2   1922   (*Castagnola*) collection Barbara Hepworth

3   *c.* 1927–28   (*still life with fruit*) collection Winifred Nicholson

4   c. 1928–29   (*Tindal Fell, Cumberland*) collection Jake Nicholson

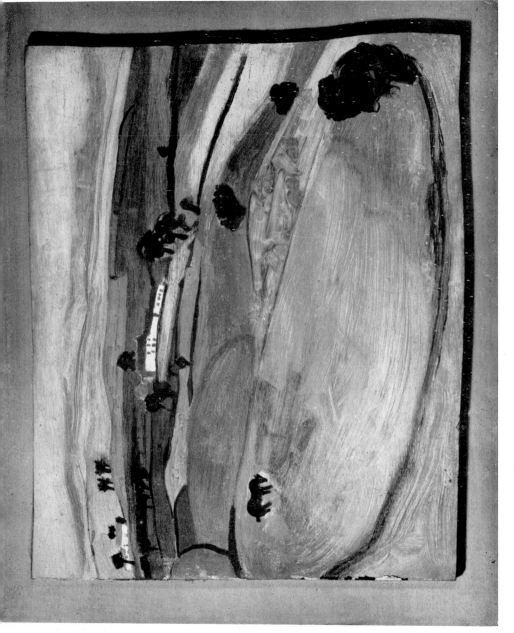

5   1930   *(Clark's Hill, Cumberland)* collection C. S. Reddihough

6   1928   (*Cumbrian landscape*) collection Tate Gallery

7 c. 1929 (fireworks) private collection London

8 1929 (*Sweaites, Cumberland*) collection Kate Nicholson

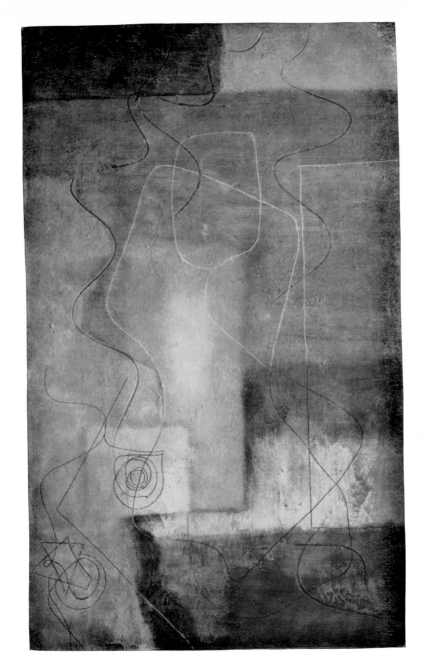

9   1932   (*figure*) collection Barbara Hepworth

10 1930 (*still life with horse*) collection Toronto Art Gallery

11   *c.* 1927   (*bottle and fruit*) collection Winifred Nicholson

12   1932   (*Talc de Coty*) collection Margaret Gardiner

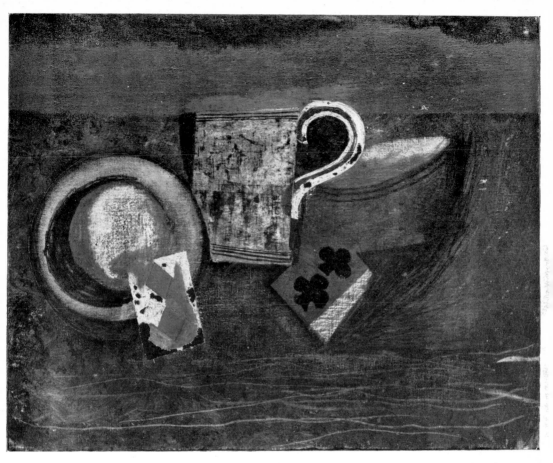

13 1930 *(still life)* collection John Aldridge

14 1932 (*violin*) collection R. H. M. Ody

15   1933   (*St. Remy, Provençe*) private collection London

17 1934 (*relief, five circles*)
destroyed

16 1940 (*bus ticket*)
collection S. & J. L. Martin

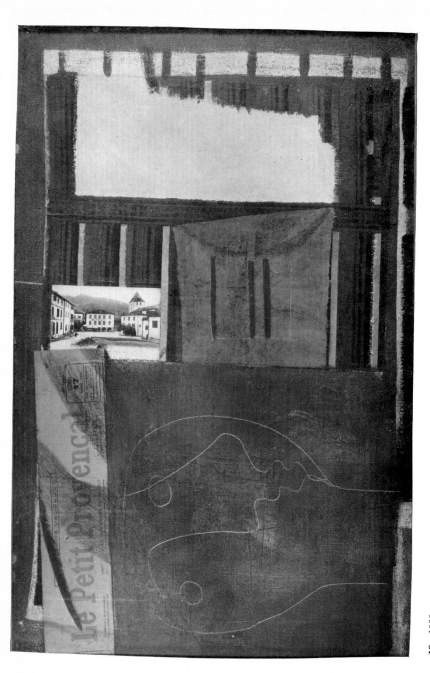

18 1933 (*collage with Spanish postcard*) collection Herbert Read

19 1932 *(musical instrument)* collection Barbara Hepworth

20 1934 (*white relief*) collection Helen Sutherland

21   June 1947   *(lilac and goblet)* collection F. L. S. Murray

23   March 1952   (*goblets on yellow ground*) collection S. & J. L. Martin

24   Oct 1949   (*cockatoo*) private collection U.S.A.

25 1946 (*goblets*) collection S. Friedman, S. Africa

26 *c.* 1938 *(white relief)*

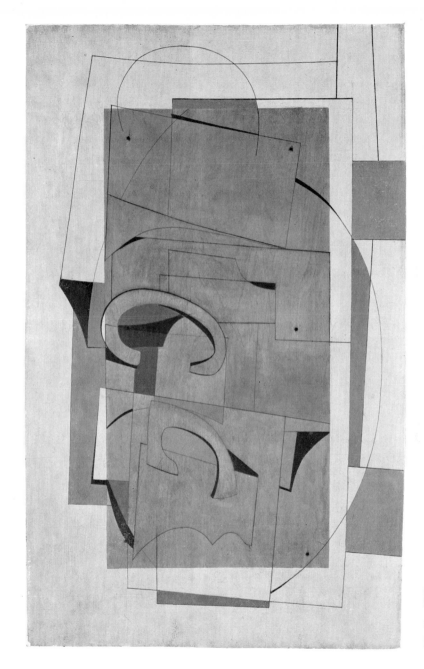

27 Oct 1951 (six eyes)

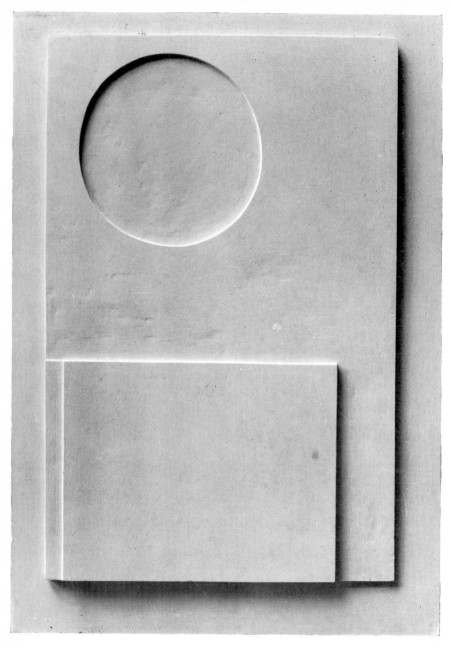

28 1935 (*white relief*) collection J. R. M. Brumwell

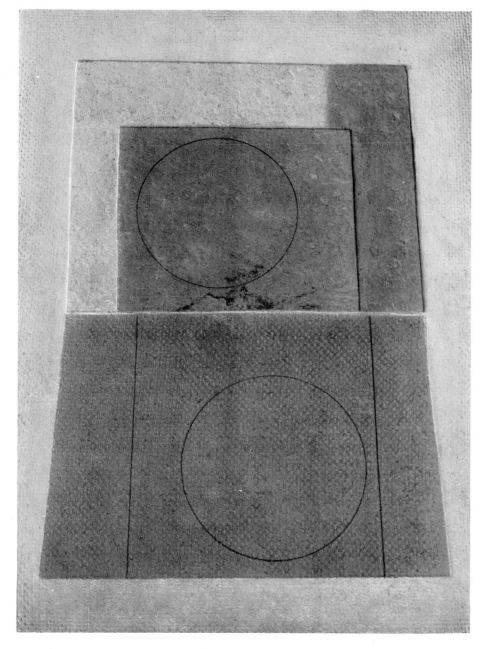

29   Feb 1956   (*Treen*) private collection U.S.A.

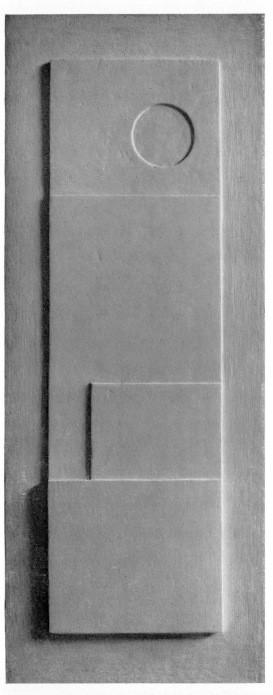

30 1934 *(white relief)*
collection Arthur Hepworth

31 Dec 1949 (*winter*)
private collection U.S.A.

32 Dec 1951
(*Greek*) private
collection U.S.A.

33 1943 (*painted relief*) private collection London

34 *c.* 1934 (*sculpture*) collection Winifred Nicholson

35 Oct 1952 *(pyramid)*

36 1956 (*single mug*) collection Simon Hepworth-Nicholson

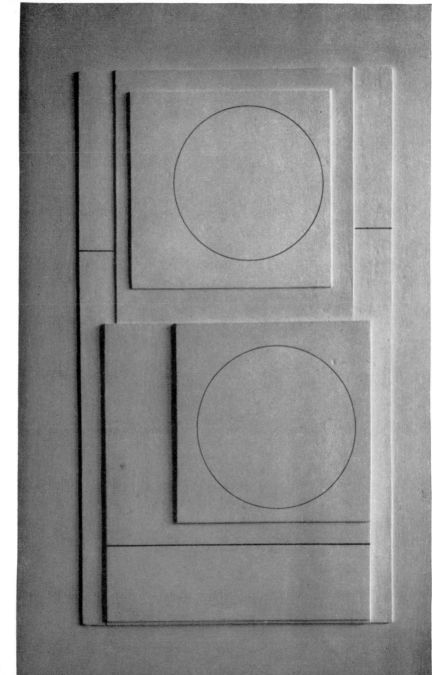

37   1941
(*white relief*)

38   Aug 1954   (*Villefranche*) collection Robert Erskine

39   Aug 1951
(*Italian still life*)
collection H. S. Ede

40 April 1953
(*three moons*)
private collection
Amsterdam

41 Jan 1948 (*Towednack*) collection C. S. Reddihough

42 Oct 1955 *(plate of pears)* collection Margaret McLeod

43 1955 (*Verona*) private collection London

44 Nov 1955 *(deep Persian lilac)* collection U.S.A.

45 Feb 1956 *(hole'd stone)*

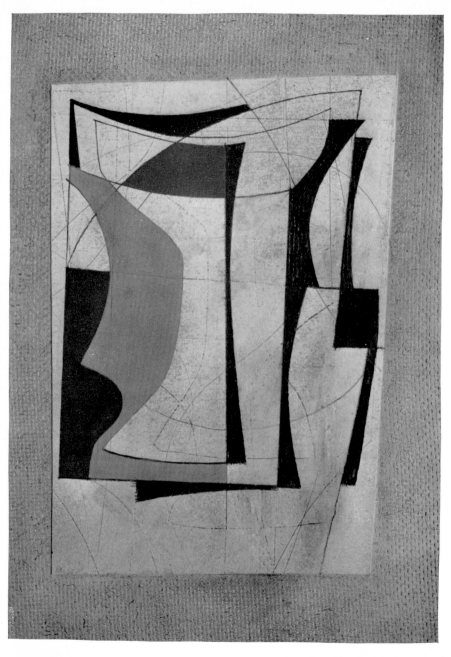

46 1955
(*sextant*) collec-
tion F. L. S.
Murray

47 April 1956 (*Tregeseal 2*) collection Herta Wescher

48   Aug 1955   (*Zennor Quoit*) collection U.S.A. (courtesy Durlacher Bros. New York)

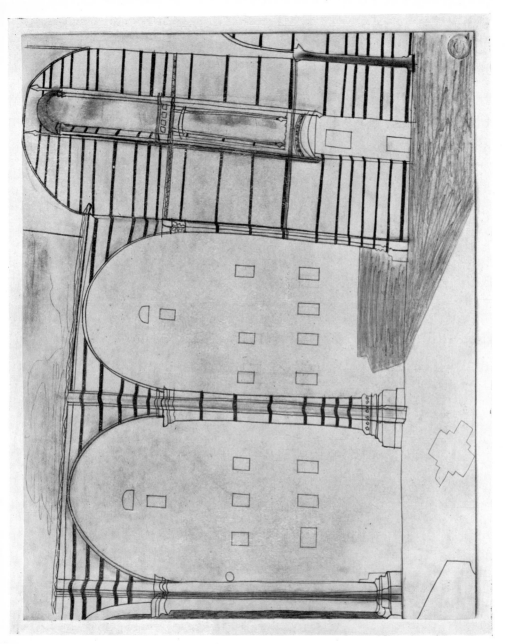

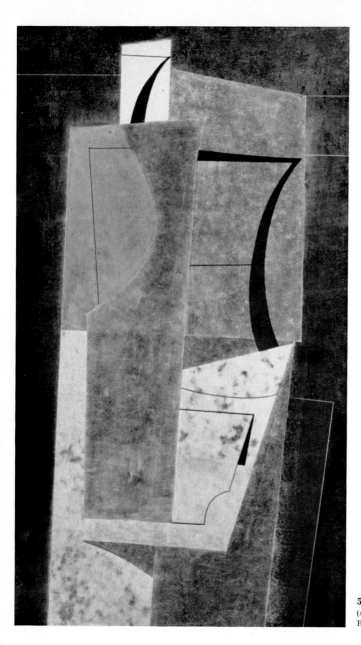

50   May 1955
(*sevenbark*) (courtesy Durlacher
Bros. New York)